TRANQUILOGY
ADULT COLORING BOOKS

CALMING ANIMAL & NATURE DESIGNS FOR
STRESS RELIEF, INSPIRATION, AND HAPPINESS

J

LIFESTYLE**DEZIGN**

LIFESTYLEDEZIGN

Lifestyle Dezign Coloring is located in Phoenix, AZ.

Proudly printed in the United States of America

It's as Easy As 1, 2, 3...

1 **De-stress: Find somewhere quiet, calming, and distraction free.**

2 **Detox from Digitals: Turn off all electronics and place them out of sight or in another room.**

3 **Design: Pull out your colored pencils or crayons, relax, be inspired, and let your imagination run wild.**

Happy Coloring!

"Our deepest fear is not that we are inadequate.
Our deepest fear is that we are powerful beyond measure.
It is our light, not our darkness, that most frightens us.
Your playing small does not serve the world.
There is nothing enlightened about shrinking so that other
people won't feel insecure around you.
We are all meant to shine as children do.
It's not just in some of us; it is in everyone.
And as we let our own lights shine, we unconsciously give other
people permission to do the same.
As we are liberated from our own fear, our presence
automatically liberates others."

- Marianne Williamson

"Quiet the mind and the soul will speak."

- Ma Jaya Sati Bhagavati

"Where there is love, there is life."

- Mohandas Gandhi

"Do something today that your future self will thank you for."

- Unknown

"You can't stop the waves, but you can learn to surf."

- Joseph Goldstein

"You are exactly who & what & where you are supposed to be and you are lovely."

- Unknown

"I am too positive to be doubtful,
too optimistic to be fearful,
and too determined to be defeated."

- Hussein Nishah

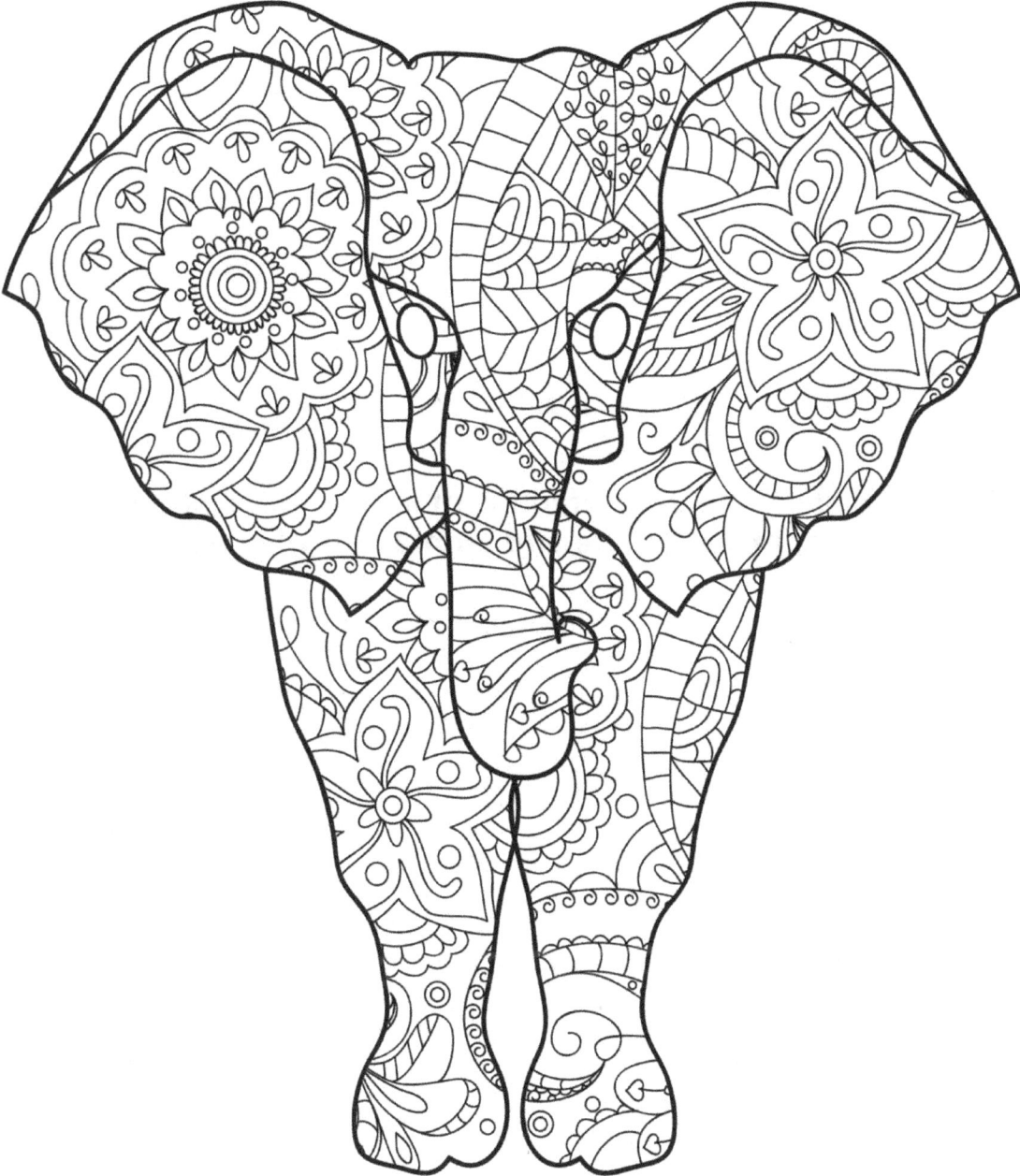

"Authenticity is the daily practice of letting go of who we think we're supposed to be and embracing who we are."

- Brene Brown

"You are never too old to set another goal or to dream a new dream."

- C.S. Lewis

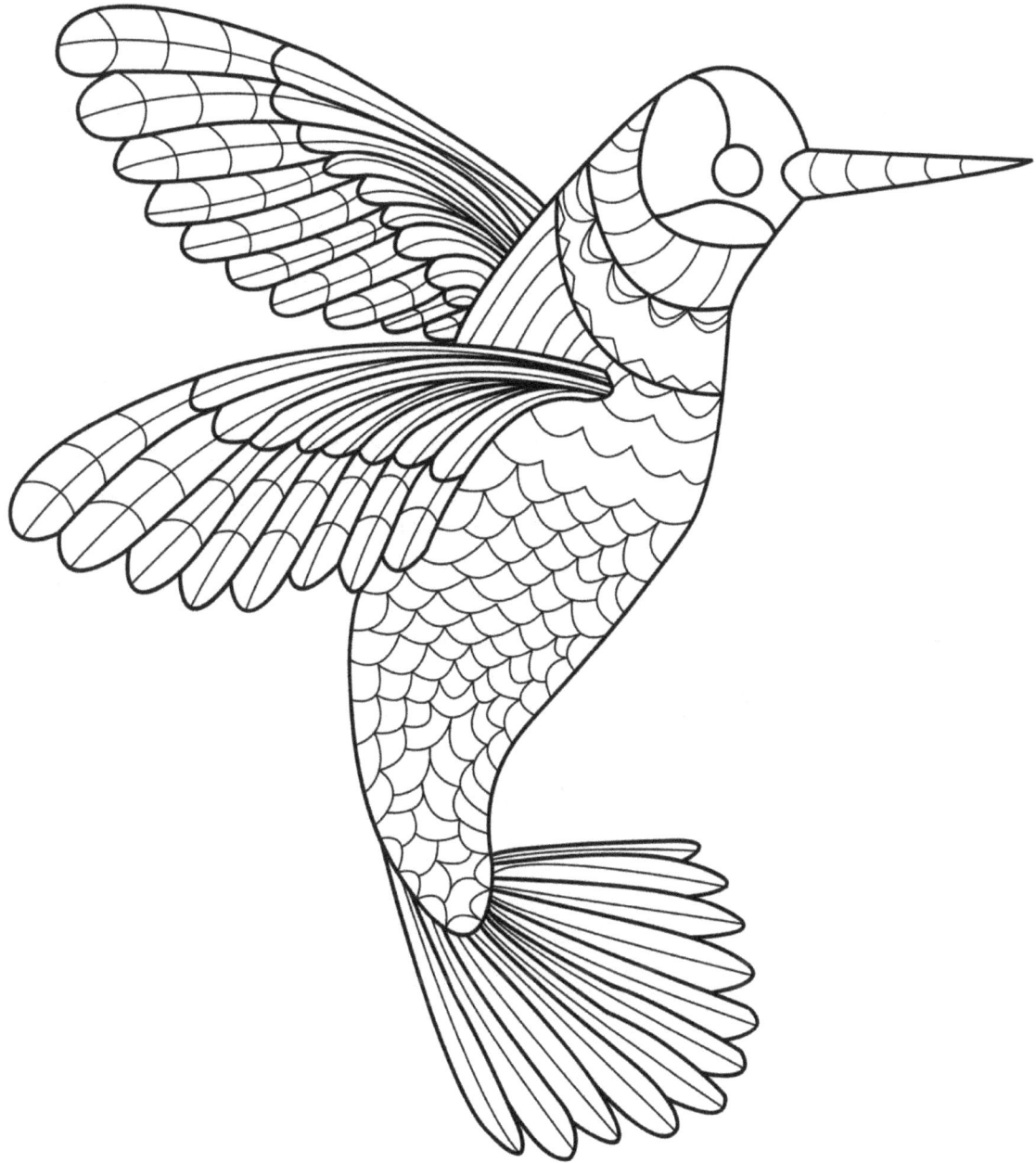

"Always remember:
You are beautiful
You are worthy
You are important
You are special
You are unique
You are wonderful
You are talented
And
You are irreplaceable"

- Unknown

"There is conditional love and unconditional love. One limits the mind, the other sets it free."

- Headspace

"I live and love with my whole heart."

- Brene Brown

"If you change the way you look at things, the things you look at change."

- Wayne Dyer

"Refuge to the man is the mind, refuge to the mind is mindfulness."

- Buddha

"It requires courage, openness, and honesty to observe the mind without judgement, criticism, or censorship."

- Headspace

"You get the best out of others when you give the best of yourself."

- Harvey S. Firestone

"Let go of comparing.
Let go of competing.
Let go of judgements.
Let go of anger.
Let go of regrets.
Let go of worrying.
Let go of blame.
Let go of guilt.
Let go of fear.
Have a proper belly laugh at least once a day."

- Unknown

"You are enough."

- Unknown

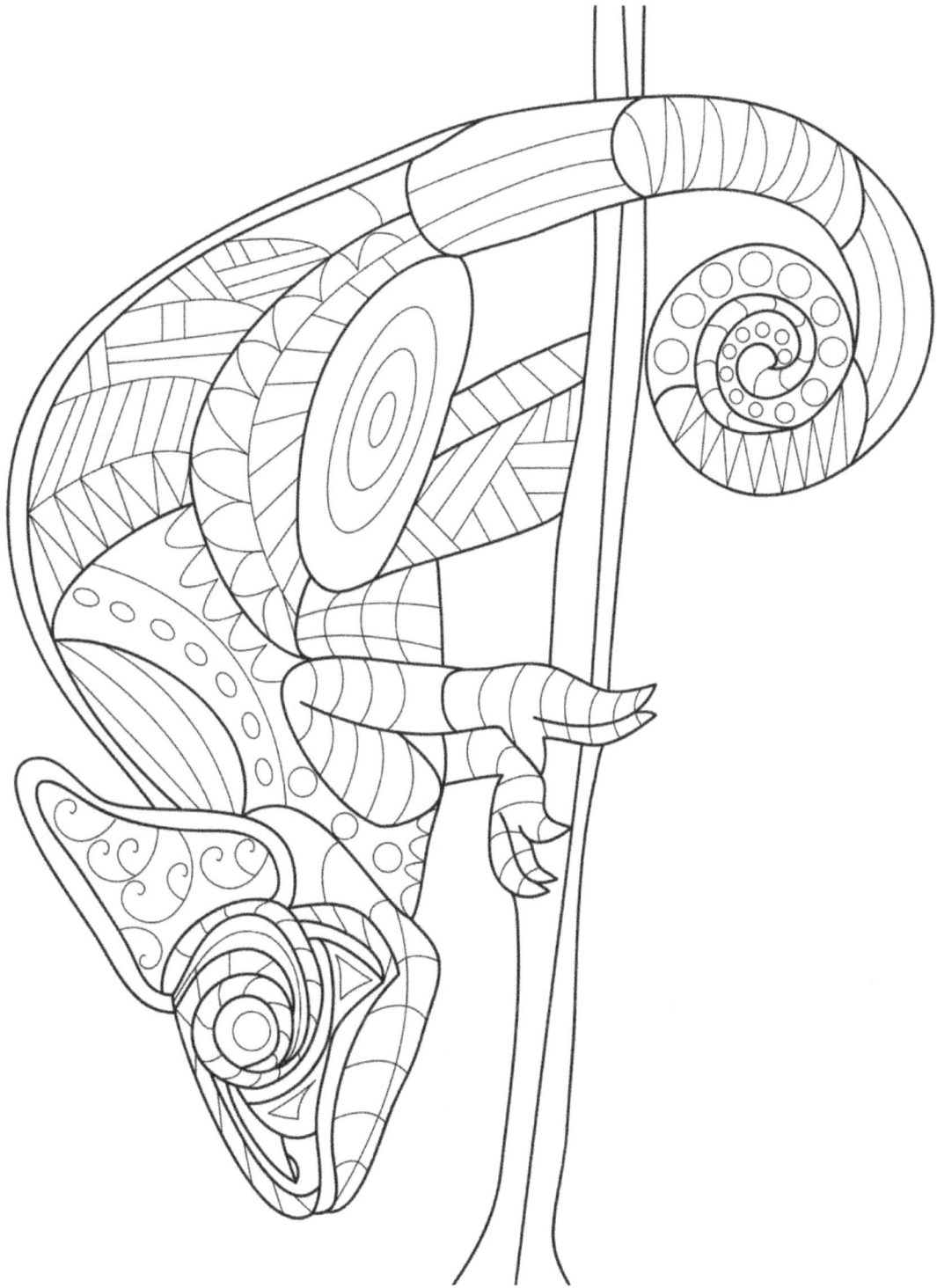

"Worthiness does not have prerequisites."

- Brene Brown

"The most precious gift we can offer others is our presence.
When mindfulness embraces those we love, they will bloom like
flowers."

- Thich Nhat Hanh

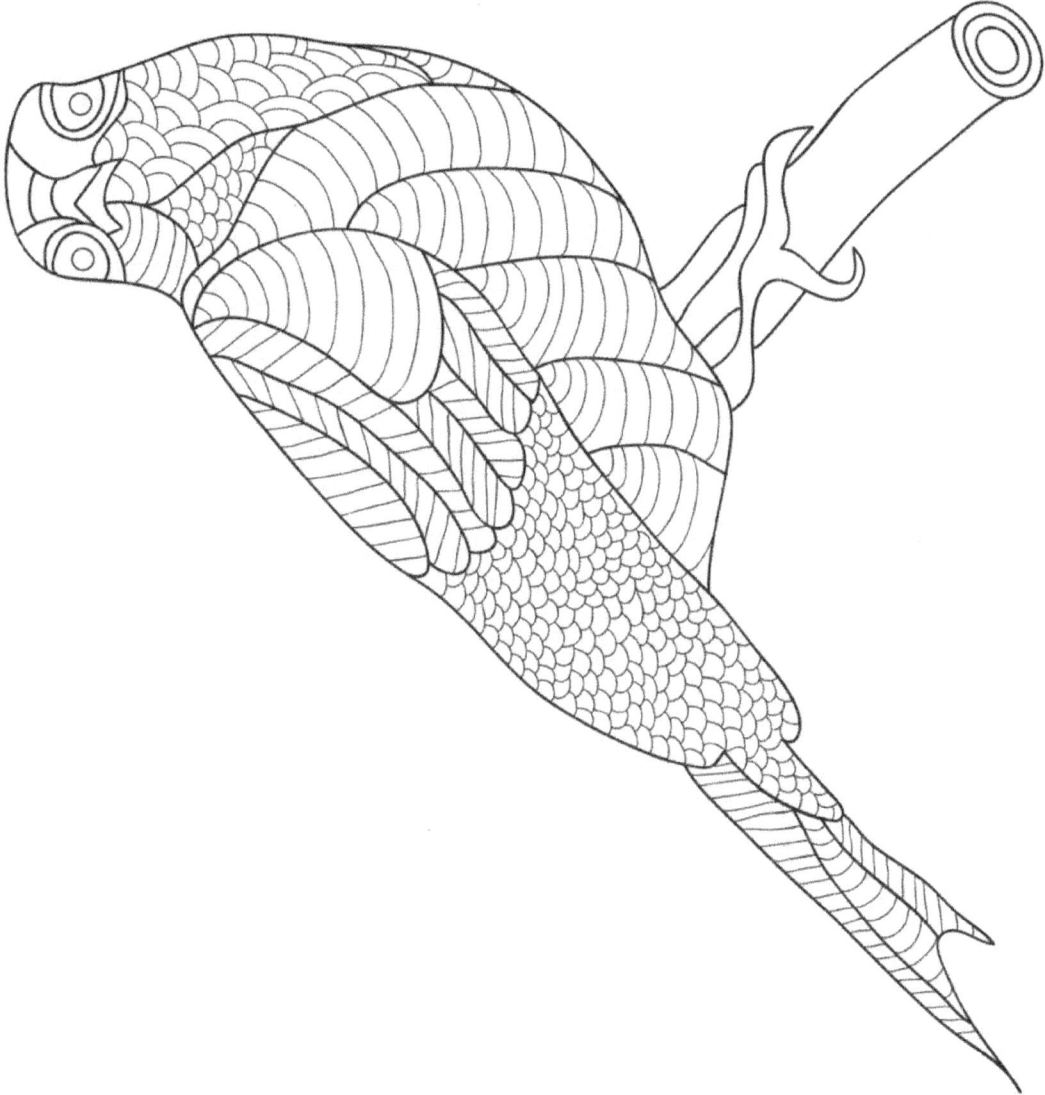

"Wherever you are, be all there."

- Jim Elliot

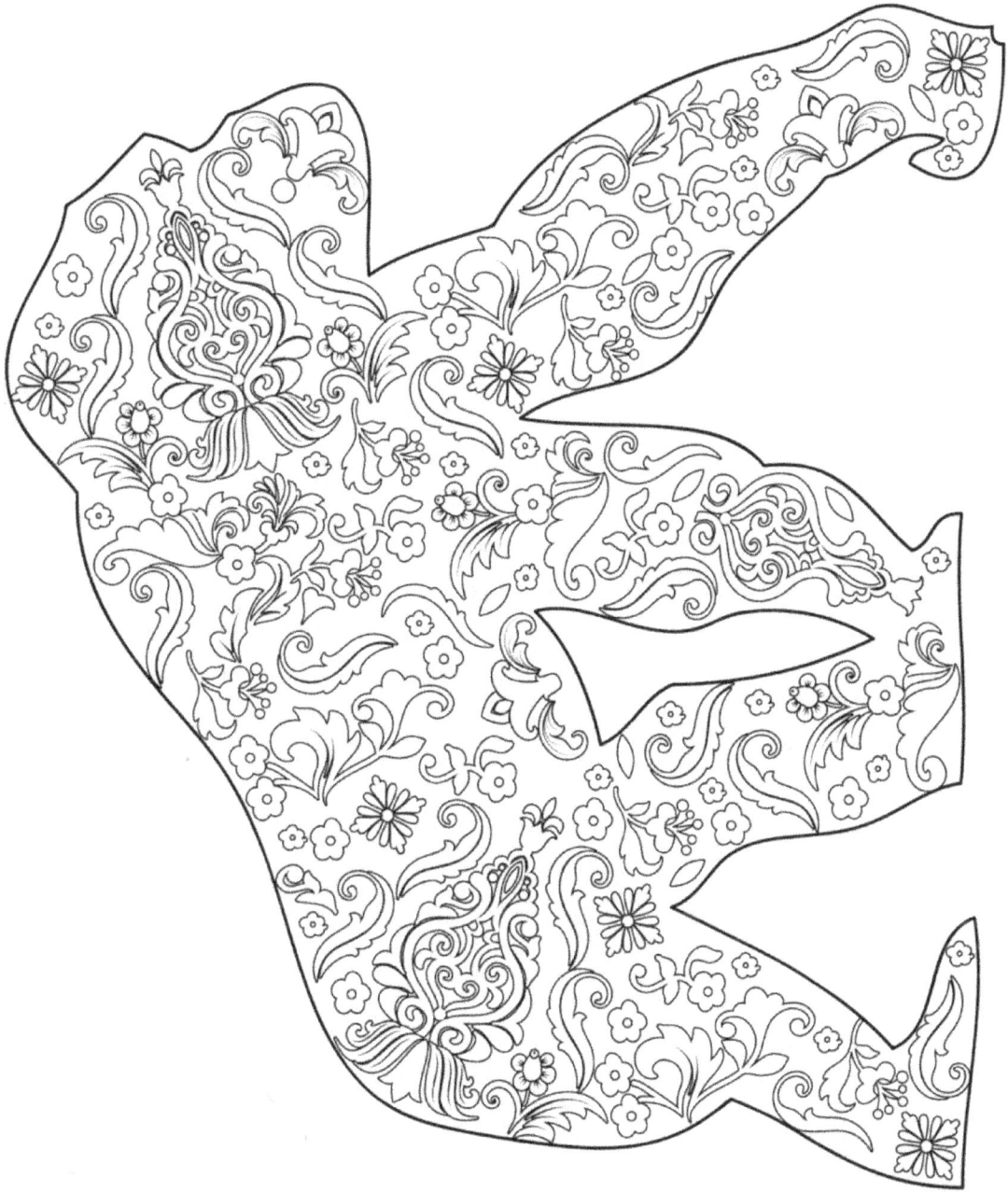

"Energy is contagious, positive and negative alike. I will forever be mindful of what and who I am allowing into my space."

- Unknown

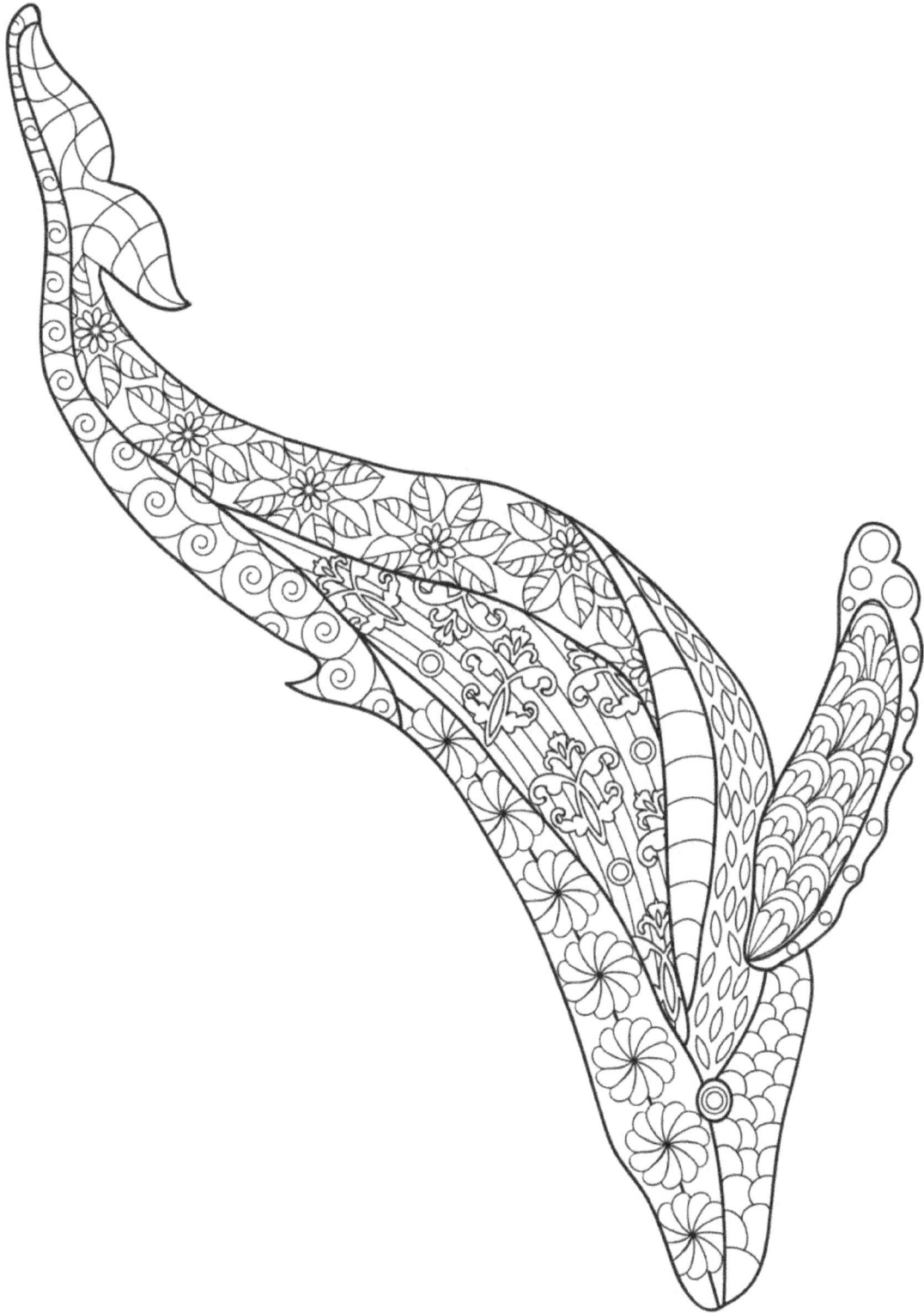

"Whether you think you can or you think you can't, you're right."

- Henry Ford

"If you're your authentic self, you have no competition."

- Scott Stratten

"To be beautiful means to be yourself. You don't need to be accepted by others. You need to accept yourself."

- Thich Nhat Hanh

"Remind yourself that it's okay not to be perfect."

- Unknown

"Life is not about waiting for the storm to pass but learning to dance in the rain."

- Vivian Greene

"Wake up every morning with the thought that something wonderful is about to happen."

- Unknown

"Nothing can bring you peace but yourself."

- Ralph Waldo Emerson

"I am not what has happened to me, I am what I choose to become."

- Carl Jung

"If you want to be sad, live in the past.
If you want to be anxious, live in the future.
If you want to be peaceful, live in the now."

- Unknown

"Don't just look, observe.
Don't just swallow, taste.
Don't just sleep, dream.
Don't just think, fell.
Don't just exist, live."

- Unknown

"Be the change you want to see in the world."

- Mahatma Gandhi

"You are worthy of love and belonging."

- Brene Brown

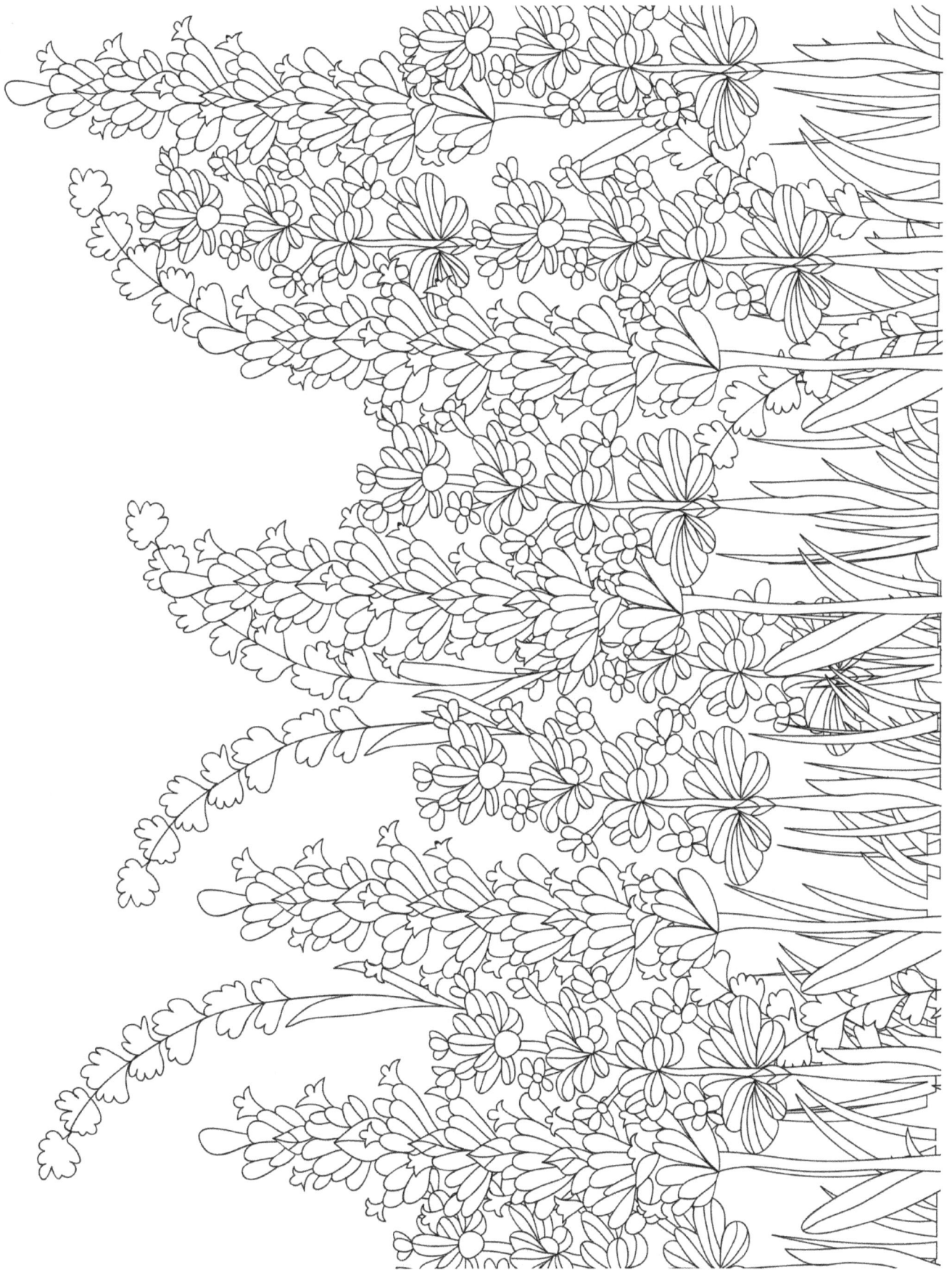

"There is no path to happiness: happiness is the path."

- Buddha

"It's not selfish to love yourself, take care of yourself, and make your happiness a priority. It's necessary."

- Mandy Hale

"Don't go where the path may lead, go instead where there is no path and leave a trail."

- Ralph Waldo Emerson

"I am in charge of how I feel and today I am choosing happiness."

- Unknown

"Being yourself is the prettiest thing you can be."

- Unknown

"Happiness does not depend on what you have or who you are.
It solely relies on what you think."

- Buddha

**"Paradise is not a place;
It's a state of consciousness."**

- Sri Chinmoy

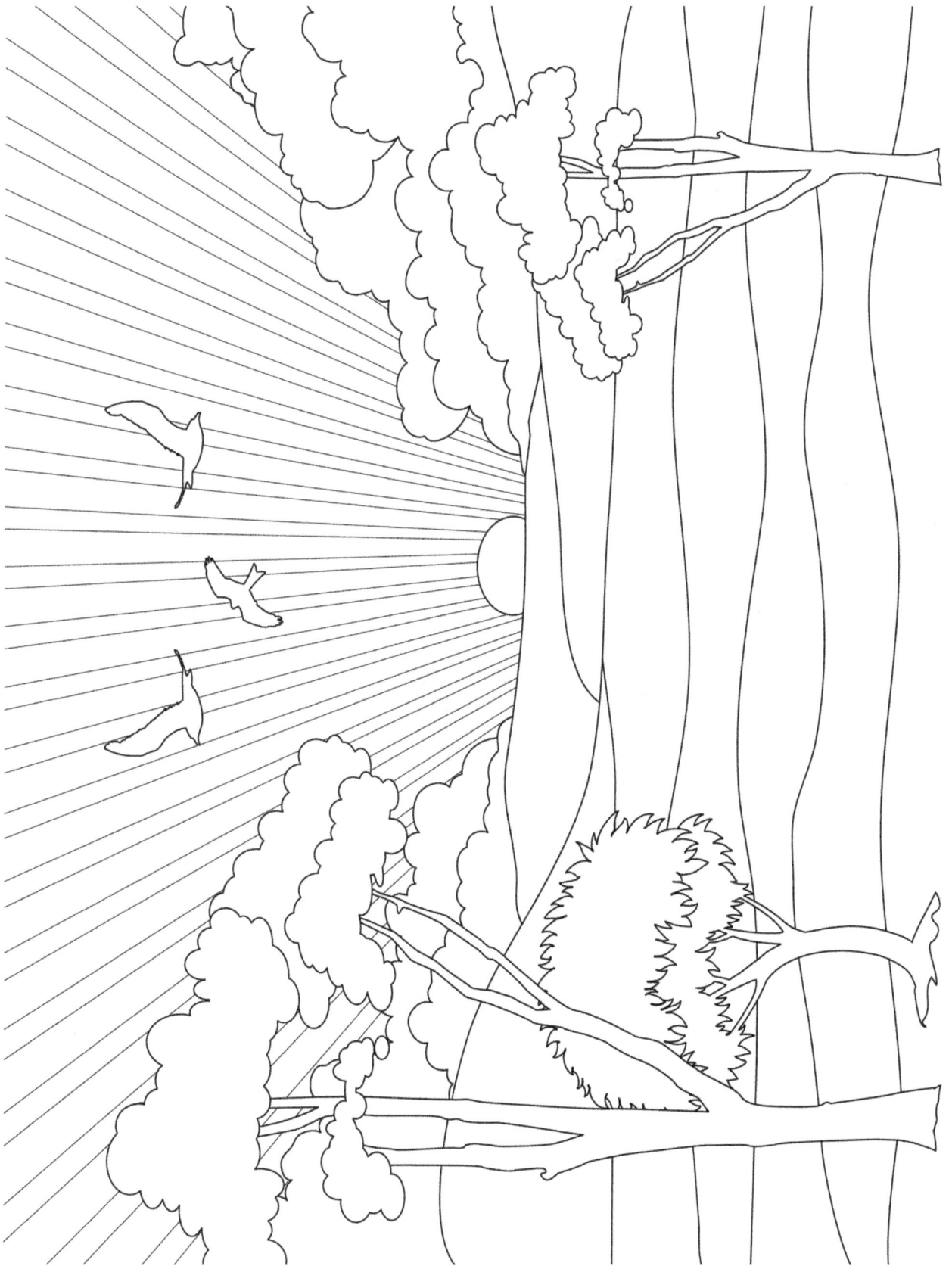

"Life is so much brighter when we focus on what truly matters."

- Zig Ziglar

"One of the happiest moments in life is when you find the courage to let go of what you can't change."

- Unknown

"Be somebody who makes everybody feel like a somebody."

- Kid President

"Our purpose is simple – to love.
To love each other,
To love all life,
And to love our earth."

- Anthony Williams

Thank you for joining the movement to bring relaxation, inspiration, and happiness into the lives of adults everywhere. Join our community of amazing colorists for tips, inspiration, to learn about our commitment to giving back, and to showcase your beautiful art!

facebook.com/lifestyledezigncoloring

@LDColoring

@lifestyledezigncoloring

pinterest.com/lifestyledezign

Now it's your turn to let your imagination go wild. Have fun drawing your own creative art and adding your illustrations to this book!

TRANQUILOGY ADULT COLORING BOOKS

TRANQUILOGY ADULT COLORING BOOKS

TRANQUILOGY ADULT COLORING BOOKS

TRANQUILOGY ADULT COLORING BOOKS

TRANQUILOGY ADULT COLORING BOOKS

www.ingramcontent.com/pod-product-compliance
Lightning Source LLC
Chambersburg PA
CBHW081218020426
42331CB00012B/3046